Yes, GOD IS TALKING TO YOU

How to Know, How to Listen

A collection of inspirational readings

MARY PHILLIPS-ASHLEY

SILVERSMITH
PRESS

Published by Silversmith Press—Houston, Texas
www.silversmithpress.com

Copyright © 2024 Mary Phillips-Ashley

All rights reserved.

To connect with the author visit yesgodistalkingtoyou.com
or email team@godistalkingtoyou.com

ISBN 978-1-961093-20-1 (Softcover Book)
ISBN 978-1-961093-21-8 (eBook)

CONTENTS

INTRODUCTION

We open the way for God's help when we take the first step. Dreams are seeds of potential waiting for you to take action. Maybe there is a dream that God has put in your heart, and you're not sure where to start. As I have learned...

Start anywhere. Just start!

That is what I did with writing this book; I just started writing. Any idea I had about prayer or intuition I wrote down. Ideas started coming to me, I believe from God, and I wrote them <u>all</u> down. That was the start. But before I started getting words on the page, I had to follow my gut, my intuition towards the direction of my dream.

Intuition can be a powerful tool in our lives if we choose to be open to it. I believe it is one of the ways God uses to answer our prayers for His direction and guidance in our lives. I never questioned it; I just acted on it immediately, and it turned out to be a wonderful blessing.

This is where my introduction becomes part story about how intuition led me to the person that would, for a short time, help me birth my dream. I believe there is someone out there to help you take your first steps in realizing your dream as well. The person I am talking about became my writing coach, Maryann. My experience with Maryann was quite different, to say the least: my intuition had to seemingly fight its way through. For some reason, I didn't immediately act on the idea to approach Maryann about my writing, and I'm not sure why. Typically, when I ask God for help with something, I make it a point to be very aware and alert to anything that might be an answer; I don't want to miss anything. My experience with Maryann was not one of those times. Let me explain.

My desire to write had started years before, and, occasionally, I *would* do some writing, yet I always felt my writing lacked direction. The desire to write was never far from my thoughts, so I finally made a conscious decision that now was the time to get serious.

I knew I needed help from someone who could work with me on developing the right format for my style of writing. I needed help in refining my ideas. I needed help with the beginning of my stories, the middle, and the end. I needed help to keep my brain from bursting.

Maryann, a fellow Prayer Chaplain, kept coming to mind. I had known her for some years, yet not very well. I knew she did life coaching, just not to what extent. I had been a small help to her some years previously, as she had been very involved with a Unity conference that had been held in Detroit, but other than that, we weren't well acquainted.

I had tried once before to work with a writing coach, but after meeting a couple of times, it just didn't feel right. After a while, someone suggested a writer and editor to consult. I talked with her about what I was looking for, yet that didn't work out either.

Once again, the idea of approaching Maryann kept coming to mind. This intuition in the back of my mind was not giving up, so I decided that, if circumstances were right, I would talk to her the following Sunday. I had mentioned to a few people about how I wanted to do some writing, so I knew she was vaguely aware.

We both tended to sit in the same area for church services; sometimes sitting together. But we did not sit together that day, and I didn't see her anywhere. Fear was already rearing its ugly head. Maybe I was wrong; maybe I was reading too much into why I believed her name kept coming to mind. I continued watching for her as people were leaving the sanctuary after service, and still, no Maryann. Okay, I was wrong; there was nothing in all these thoughts I was having about her.

I turned the corner, and she found me—just came right up and started talking. I was proud of myself; I didn't hesitate. I jumped right in and told her what I had been thinking, and, on the spot, she agreed to be my coach. It began right there with her giving me much encouragement and very good advice. The idea that this might work was both exhilarating and terrifying. After finally following that intuition and talking with her, I truly believed this was the right next step for me.

Talking with her made all the possibilities feel more real, which brought on more doubts about what I was doing. People might actually read my words! And what would they think? Would they say, "What right does she have to think her opinions are valuable?" and so on?

We only worked together for a short time, and it was a few months after that when I realized what I had learned from our time together.

INTRODUCTION, PART 2

When Maryann and I started, I had pages and pages of thoughts and ideas, but nothing was put together in any sense of a format or logical sequence. It was almost embarrassing to have someone else read all my hodgepodge, trying to make something out of it. We worked together only a short time, and I was feeling a little confused about the intuition that had led me to her in the first place. I couldn't see what had come of it, at least not right away. I just wasn't getting anywhere, so we stopped.

I continued writing, but I kept feeling a little discouraged and not knowing where this was going. A few months later, right after I had finished reading a book by Florence Scovil Shin, it occurred to me how much I enjoyed her writing. She often used examples of her own experiences to get a point across, and that is when it hit me. I could use the format of telling short stories to say what I wanted to say, use my experiences of answered prayer, big or small, to help others recognize God working in *their* lives. WOW! This was big; this was what I had been looking for and didn't know it. I believe I would not have discovered this without the time I had spent with Maryann. She helped me see that what I had to say could be of value to others, and, with her help, I was able to get past my own insecurities and start to move forward.

I hope the stories that follow will help you discover that God has always been there and that He cares about you! He wants to be involved in your everyday life, if you will just invite Him in.

May His "goodness and blessings follow you all the days of your life and may you dwell in the house of the Lord forever" (Psalm 23:6).

Chapter 1

STAY OPEN TO NEW IDEAS

One of my favorite stories of answered prayer and following intuition is the one about how I became an assistant to Reverend Sandy Hess. Rev. Hess, now retired, was one of the ministers at the Unity Church I attend. One of her many jobs was to oversee the Prayer Chaplain team. As a member of that team, I got to know her pretty well and had many opportunities to experience her deep faith in God, her ability to give to others, and her wonderful sense of humor. It was a joy to be with her.

My story starts with my desire to do more in the way of volunteering. I was unclear just what that might be, yet the desire was strong. It all started when I was listening to a webinar given by Neale Donald Walsh, the author of the *Conversations with God* series of books. He is one of my favorite writers, and this series has had a profound effect on my life. His subject that day was volunteer service. He spoke of the importance of serving and helping others, which usually ends up helping ourselves as well. I was already volunteering as a Prayer Chaplain at my church, which I very much enjoyed. In our service as Chaplains, we not only pray with congregants after Sunday service; we also help with the many events that take place at any church: funerals, weddings, special events, and the like. At this time, I was no longer working and, in the back of my mind, had been thinking of doing more, of being more involved. So, I prayed about it and asked God for guidance. Within a very short period of time, an amazing idea came to me: I could be an assistant to Rev. Hess! From heaven above, this idea seemed to fill my mind. Such a thought had never occurred to me before, yet I instantly liked the idea. Rev. Hess' assistant—I could do that! I had no idea what might be involved. I just knew it felt right. The thought that she may already have an assistant, or possibly didn't need or even want one, never entered my mind. I was far too enthusiastic for such details.

I decided to approach her the following Sunday, and I could hardly wait. Anyone who knows me well can attest to what I can be like when I get excited about an idea: Stand back! I could barely sit still during the Sunday service. Once I saw her sitting across the way, I knew that day was the day. I found her immediately after the service talking with some of the other Prayer Chaplains. I walked right up and declared: "Rev. Hess, I'm going to be your new assistant!" That was all I said. Just a little taken aback, she said, "Okay." We talked a few minutes and decided I would start that week, just two or three days a week, doing whatever it was she needed me to do.

I had never dreamed I'd be working with her before that intuition came to me. The fact that she was thrilled to have me made it even better. Others had offered to be her assistant. For whatever reason, she had always turned them down, yet she accepted me immediately.

Truth be told, I didn't give her much of a choice. I believed this would be a perfect arrangement for both of us, and so it was. The way all of this fell into place helped me get a better understanding of how the universe works to provide everyone with what they need. It was about more than just my life. I filled a need for her that I didn't know existed at the time, and it filled my desire to do more in the way of volunteering.

It turned out to be a wonderful experience for both of us. We were a perfect fit; we worked well together, and our personalities complemented each other, which truly made every moment a joy. We could laugh and find fun in the most mundane activities. Our laughter would often bring others out of their office in to see what was going on. Since neither one of us was a pro on the computer, I would laugh with delight after figuring out some difficult task. It just added to the fun and amusement as we worked diligently to accomplish that day's goals and the fun we had made every day a joy.

This truly was one of those times when following my intuition became a gift from God (or whatever you choose to call it). For me, it was a miracle. God knew what Rev. Hess needed, and God knew what I needed. Because I chose to listen and believe, the most marvelous things took place, and we were both immensely blessed.

Father God, every day we begin anew, today I open my mind to change, to possibility, to trying something new. Even just a new thought or way of doing something can have a profound effect on my life. We don't always realize how insidious our habits are; we do something without even thinking about it. Not today—today I will try to do something new or try a different approach. Today I'll read something that challenges my thinking and see where it takes me. This is where we find our true joy, where we live life as it was meant to be lived. We thank You God, for the variety You have given us in every aspect of life. Today I will appreciate it more by searching out something new. We are so grateful, in Jesus' name we pray, Amen.

Chapter 2

LET GO OF WHATS NOT WORKING

For various reasons, most of us have specific ideas about how the answers to our prayers should look, and if what we receive does not look as we think it should, we may not believe our prayers have been answered. How many times have we prayed about a matter and told God exactly what we want, when it should happen, and where, and that is all we'll accept? As a Prayer Chaplain for many years, the training I have received has helped me understand how we can limit how our prayers are answered by not being open to possibilities. So often it turns out that we are quite glad that something we prayed about did not turn out the way we hoped it would. Experiences like that help take off whatever "limits" our own thinking has put on God. This story is about how I "let" God find the perfect job for me, with just one or two limits.

Several years ago, I decided it was time for a job change. I didn't know what I wanted to do or where I wanted to work, just that I was not happy where I was. At the time, I was working in the office of a very small company that was not yet using computers, which was fine with me. It was the first time I had ever worked in an office; before that job, all my work experience was in the retail industry, which had not involved using a computer. Even though I did have one at home, I didn't use it much. It was my belief that I needed to find a place that would give me on-the-job computer training. I had taken a few computer courses over the years, and as they say, "use it or lose it." Without somewhere to use it, I did lose what I had learned.

So, I made the decision to put it all in God's hands. All I asked for in my prayer was a place that would be willing to give me on-the-job computer training, and I left the rest open to God. I let all my friends know that I was job-hunting, and then I waited. I would look in the paper and online from time to time to see what was out there, but nothing seemed right.

During that time, my friend Nina helped me realize that if I wanted a job with a different vibe from where I was, it might help if I did a little work on my attitude. I was very critical of my boss and the way things were done. Nina pointed out that if I wanted the next situation to be more to my liking, I was the one who needed to change. I needed to find some positive ways to think about my present boss, and it wouldn't be easy.

So, over the next several days, I went to work on it in my head. I was trying to find something positive about her that I believed was true and that would help me eliminate all the negative energy that I had created around the situation. It sounds terrible to me that finding a positive thought was so difficult. I could come up with a few things about the job I liked: good hours, time off when needed, close to home. I used these for a while to build up my good will, yet I still felt I would like to be able to see my boss in a better light. The best I could come up with was "She's doing the best she can." That was it, and that was what I used. Whenever negative thoughts would come to mind, I would push them away and focus on the idea, "She's doing the best she can." It didn't take long for me to start seeing her with more understanding eyes. I knew a little about her past, and her life had not been easy, so I used that to help me stay on target.

About a month went by, and I received a call from an acquaintance who told me about a friend of hers who needed an office assistant in a small family business. She gave me a name and number, and I made the call. I was pretty nervous; I hadn't been job-hunting in years, but I dove right in. I thought it went very well and was quite pleased by how the conversation turned out. They, too, seemed pleased and said they would be calling back to arrange an interview. My hopes were high, and I thought I would hear from them within a few days, but time went by, and I heard nothing. I was sure that, for some reason, it hadn't gone as well as I had imagined and started feeling very discouraged.

It was a long two weeks before they called back and an interview was finally arranged. Once I met with them, I was again very happy with how things seemed to be going. My lack of computer skills was not an issue; in fact, they saw my willing attitude as more important. Again, my hopes were high, and by this time, I had made huge strides in aligning my thinking more positively towards my "soon-to-be" former boss, yet it seemed I still had some progress yet to make.

Again, it was a few weeks before I heard from them, which at the time made me wonder if it would work out after all. I didn't know how to interpret their lack of communication, and my mind immediately went to thoughts of "there must be something wrong with me." At that point, I had myself on quite a roller coaster, up and down, up and down. I didn't even consider the idea that since they were looking for help it might mean it was a very busy time for them, which turned out to be the case.

During the wait, I had talked to a close friend, Marissa, about the interview and how I was feeling very hopeful. We hadn't seen each other in some time, so she suggested meeting for dinner, with my husband, Art, and her husband, Paul. As the evening went on, Paul asked about the interview and what kind of job it was. I told him all about it being a small family office, and I mentioned the family's last name. What a surprise, Paul had known this family most of his life! They had lost touch over the years, and Paul was glad to hear they were still in the area. He told me to give him as a reference and to make sure I let them know he would love to get in touch.

Finally, they called again, and a second interview was arranged. It went extremely well, and once I told them about knowing Paul and his saying I could use him for a reference. The job was mine!

God had brought me to a place that turned out to be a perfect fit for all involved. I stayed there more than five years, and when I left, I took my computer skills with me! I prayed about it; I worked on the issues that were brought to my attention and let God take care of the rest. What a lesson in trusting God's ways and God's timing.

Father God, we take it all in when we hear about answered prayers. We ponder over it in our hearts and minds to firm up and know that You are always paying attention to each one of us. We build on what we see every day, prayers being heard, and prayers being answered. It's both humbling and exciting to see Your blessings flow and Your power in action. Let us not lose the awe we feel at the amazing work You are doing in our lives. Thank you, God. In Jesus' name, Amen.

Chapter 3

YOUR THOUGHTS
MAKE A DIFFERENCE

This next story is about one of the many times I have taken my granddaughter, Jenna, shopping. Jenna is one of the grandchildren I was happily blessed with when I married my husband, Art. I am now blessed to have ten grandchildren. Jenna was the third grandchild and the first granddaughter. She and I both love to shop, so whenever we're together, there is sure to be at least one shopping excursion.

Jenna and her family were here for a visit, and even though it was just for a short weekend, we made sure to get in a trip to the local mall. Jenna was seventeen at the time and in her last year of high school. She had just taken on a new part-time job, and of course, a few new "work" outfits were a must. So, off to the shops we went. One of her favorite stores was first on our list. As we walked through the store chatting about this and that, we found the perfect items for a teenager starting a new job.

Once we got back to the house, we sat down and examined all our wonderful finds. The perfect end to a fun afternoon. Jenna and her family headed for home the next day.

I found myself at that same mall a few days later, and as I was walking by the store where we had made most of her purchases, I noticed a sign displayed in the window: "40% Off Everything." You can guess where my mind went then. I was pretty sure there were no sales going on the day we were there. I didn't know for sure, and I was feeling quite perturbed. I had spent a good amount of money in that store, so I couldn't wait to get home and look at the receipt.

When I rushed home and found it, I looked at every item; nothing had been on sale. Everything had been full price. I sat down and thought for a minute. Before I knew it, my mind was full of thoughts saying, "What do you think you can do? They'll never give you the sale prices; the clothes aren't even here to take back with the receipt." Or "The items you bought are probably not even included in the sale." I had to stop myself right there.

I consider myself a positive thinker, and I was a little shocked to find my mind going off in this direction. Okay, I had to talk to myself and nip this in the bud. I did a complete "180" and chose the thoughts I would have. "I will call the store and talk to a kind, patient, considerate salesperson. I will explain the situation, and they will offer me the sale price on all the items I bought. Okay, I can do this." I made the call. The person who answered was not at all helpful, and she would not commit to saying that I would be able to receive the sale price. *Not off to a good start*, I thought.

Nevertheless, I headed for the store with my receipt in hand. I was determined to be kind and polite and to not go in with an angry attitude. I would be sweet as pie, believing they would try to work with me. I walked up to the counter, smiling all the way, and told the salesperson my story. "No problem, I can do that for you right now." Yes, this was what I wanted, and I believe that changing my thoughts, if nothing else, made the whole process easier.

So, how is your thinking when you need to deal with a similar situation? Do you take your thoughts by the hand and choose how you'll handle a situation? Or are your thoughts in charge of you?

Father God, when I find myself struggling with what is, I realize it's time to check in with my own thinking. I take the time to look more closely at where my thoughts are taking me and see where adjustments can be made in how I'm viewing a situation. Sometimes just acknowledging that I don't want to stay on the path I'm taking can be enough to make a shift and realign my thinking. In prayer, I turn it over to You, knowing and trusting all is well. Thank you, God. In Jesus' name, Amen.

Chapter 4

EXPLORE YOUR TALENTS AND GIFTS

Do you have a hobby? Something that you're good at and just enjoy doing? I have two special hobbies: I write poetry and I'm a quilter. I don't remember how the poetry came about, but I do enjoy it. Some of my favorite poems are ones I have written for friends to celebrate certain special occasions in their lives. When I was still working, some of my best poems were written for people in the office: simple, amusing verses describing someone's birthday or other event. Many times when my husband and I host Christmas parties, I'll write a poem, using the names of all our guests, depicting activities and all the things that need to get done leading up to Christmas. It's so much fun to read them aloud and hear everyone laugh as they hear their names in one of my poems.

As far as getting interested in quilting, that's a story all its own; let me tell you how that came about.

Before I decided to give quilting a try, I had been experimenting with all sorts of things. I was searching for some kind of artistic expression that I hoped was somewhere deep within me, LOL. Not really; I just wanted a hobby other than poetry but that would still be creative and something I would find interesting and fun.

Since I didn't know where to start, I made the decision to try some classes in anything that hit my fancy. I started by looking in the directory of the local community college, which offered a huge variety of classes to pick from. The first one that stood out to me was flower arranging: how hard could that be? The next class started in a couple of weeks, and I was there. It sounds simple enough; you take something that is already beautiful and try to create a display that will enhance its beauty. I found it quite embarrassing looking at the mess I would come up with and then seeing the works of art that others in the class were able to create.

I had no idea it would be so hard, at least it was for me. Maybe hard isn't the correct word; I just had no aptitude for flower arranging. I stuck it out for the whole six weeks, hoping I might learn something and get better, but I never did. Other students were already talking about the advanced class and didn't even mention it to me. It was obvious to everyone that flower arranging was not my forte. So much for that!

Next, I took a mandala class. Mandalas are intricate, geometric designs that are meant to represent the universe in the Buddhist religion. The idea is to draw these intricate designs using colored pencils on black paper, letting the unconscious mind within us take hold and lead our drawing. I would get started, then not like how it was going and start over. Over and over and over. I didn't do well at that either. My conscious mind didn't seem to understand the concept of letting the unconscious mind take over and express itself.

Next came one-stroke painting. The teacher showed us how she had turned plain glass and baskets into beautiful works of art by this method. When the strokes are put together you end up with pretty flowers, sunsets, or stunning scenes that can be painted on whatever you choose. Yet, again, it was not meant for me. My sister would always say that I couldn't even paint a wall. I thought because this was so much smaller it would be easy. Wrong again.

Many classes followed, all with the same result; I just wasn't finding anything that really spoke to me and that I was good at. I even gave Sweet Adelines a try. They are an all-women singing group with chapters all over the country. They are very involved in competitions and travel all over the state to compete against other chapters. Along with the almost-daily rehearsals, it was more than I wanted.

I was feeling very discouraged, and that's when a friend told me about quilting. Geri had been quilting for many years, and her quilts were truly works of art. I had never considered quilting, even though sewing was one thing I did well. Years ago, I had made almost all of my own clothes. I had even made a suit for my husband. Sewing a straight line: I could do this. What has turned out to be the only problem for me is choosing fabric from the thousands of beautiful designs and colors. Every quilt store I go to is different from the last, each displaying already-made quilts, which fill my mind with thoughts of "I could make that." Let the shopping begin: something else I'm very good at.

Geri, who started it all, has become a very good friend and teacher and is always there if I need help. I am not one to always follow a pattern, designing as I go along, which isn't always the best idea. Geri has often found me at her door with the beginning of something that I hope will turn into a quilt, and she's never failed to help me figure out what to do next.

I have been quilting now for many years, and it has turned out to be the perfect hobby for me. I've had some of my quilts in shows and marvel at some of the beautiful work I've seen done by others. There are always new fabrics and patterns to try, and it's a joy to come up with my own creations. I never find it boring, and I believe it is one of the gifts God has given me.

Father God, we celebrate who we are, and who You have created us to be. The biggest gift we can give ourselves is accepting who we are, embracing all that makes us unique. Developing our own gifts and talents and using them can bring us deep satisfaction as it brings us closer to You. With our unique abilities, we each have something special to give to the world and sharing who we are gives us true joy. We thank you God as we discover the talents and blessings You have put within each one of us. We are so grateful for these gifts. In Jesus' name we pray, Amen.

Chapter 5

LISTEN TO HEAR
GOD'S VOICE

A still, small voice. That is how I've often heard intuition described, a voice that is heard from within. I've heard it many times, and I usually follow it, especially when it's sounding a warning. This time, it came through loud and clear, very distinct, and I responded immediately. Let me tell you about it.

I was out walking my dog one evening. I live on somewhat of a small peninsula that juts out into Lake St. Clair, which is northeast of Detroit and borders on Canada. There is only one road that circles around the area; it goes to the right or to the left. My dog at that time was Sadie, who was a rescued dog, and she was the one who usually picked which way we would go, and this evening, she decided we would be going right. A short distance from my house, there is a large planting of arborvitae bushes that make it difficult to see that the road veers off to the left. The turn is so sharp you can't see around the bushes until you are almost past them. My usual course, whenever we are approaching this turn, is to walk almost in the middle of the street, since there are no sidewalks. Doing that makes it possible to see if a car may be coming and to make sure they can see me.

On this particular evening as we were approaching the turn, I heard a voice from within me coming through loud and clear, "Get out of the street; go beside the bushes onto the grass." From that position, I can't see around the turn, and no one can see me, but it is out of the street. And so, I did what the voice told me to do, and I did it quickly.

Just as we were stepping onto the grass, I could hear the roar of a car coming, and it was coming fast! Because you can't see around this turn, most drivers tend to slow down a little, but this car just kept on coming at full speed. By the time it got to where the driver would have been able to see us, there would not have been time for us to get out of the way or for it to slow down and not run right into us! I watched the car go by from the safety of the grass. It continued on, the driver seemingly oblivious to us, never slowing its speed.

I've heard that voice many times before, sometimes very directly, as happened in this situation. Other times, it may be just a "suggestion," sometimes while driving, an idea to go a different way, and that is what I do. I have learned over time that the more I listen and respond, the more I become attuned to recognizing intuition and following its direction in my life.

God is speaking to all of us, all the time. Do we believe that? Do we want God involved in our lives? Are we paying attention? It is our choice and I have seen that the more I am willing to listen and receive, the more I "hear."

Father God, we look to You for direction and guidance and at the same time it is up to us to follow that direction. It is up to us to take responsibility for hearing and doing the guidance we receive, to accept all that You bless us with. We see our lives move along with much more ease when we do what is ours to do and we thank You for that. We thank You God for how much You love us and how You care for us as we strive to put into practice all Your ways for us. This we pray in Jesus' name, Amen.

Chapter 6

WHERE ARE YOU PLACING YOUR FOCUS?

What do we miss when we have a certain expectation about how a situation is supposed to turn out? How many times have we had a plan for a special day, maybe a family get-together for a holiday, and just expected, without even realizing it, that certain things would happen, and that the day would go a certain way? The following story is about the time my brother invited Art and me for Thanksgiving dinner … and it didn't go as I expected.

It was the fourth Thursday of the eleventh month of the year. It was a day, at least in my thinking, that the world should be eating turkey for dinner. My brother, Albert, and his wife, Nancy, had invited Art and me to come across the state and join them for Thanksgiving dinner. We would head their way early the morning of Thanksgiving, spend most of the day with them and the kids, and drive home the next day. I was so excited as we walked up the steps after our three-hour drive. My sister-in-law, Nancy, is a wonderful cook, and I knew everything would be delicious. All the kids would be there too, and I could barely contain myself. We knocked at the door, and I could hardly wait as the sound of footsteps told us someone was coming. One of my nieces answered the door, wearing a grin from ear to ear, and gave me a big hug, but as I stepped inside, my senses noticed something was wrong right away before I knew what it was. We continued greeting the family with hellos and hugs as if everything was normal, yet I still felt that something was amiss.

All of a sudden, I realized what it was. I love the way the whole house smells while turkey is cooking; the aroma fills every room and whets your appetite for what is to come. But as I walked around in the midst of greeting everyone, I realized I couldn't smell any turkey! How could this be? I was dumbfounded when I was told there would be no turkey for dinner. This was the fourth Thursday of the eleventh month, and we were not having turkey for dinner! I must clarify here that it is not that I love the taste of turkey so much; I normally have it maybe two or three times a year, but on this day, I expect to eat turkey! I expect the air to be filled with the aroma of turkey!

My brother had told his wife that nobody in our family liked turkey and convinced her to cook a ham instead. Ham. On Thanksgiving Day. I just don't know how he did it. Nancy is an amazing, sweet, loving person, and we have a wonderful relationship, and she had never mentioned that we would not be having turkey. Oh, of course, they had all the fixings: sweet potatoes, mashed potatoes, hot rolls, salad, several vegetables, and delicious pies for desert ... but no turkey. That was all I seemed capable of focusing on: there was to be no turkey for Thanksgiving dinner.

Alright, I know what you're probably thinking. "Give it a rest and enjoy the other wonderful things about the day." I am happy to say that eventually I did just that, but I had to keep talking myself through it, and I did finally come around.

It turned into quite a lesson about what we are focusing on, what we are giving our attention to. A lesson about awareness, being aware of our own thinking and where it may be taking us, because it can take us on a ride we may not wish to take. My thinking was doing just that by focusing on something that I felt was wrong and not seeing all the wonder of the rest of the day: being with the people I love and enjoying their company. Isn't that what it's all about when we make plans for such occasions, especially with our hectic lifestyles today? Our families and friends can be scattered all over the world, and it is often only the holidays that bring us together.

Fortunately for me, I got it together after realizing what was happening and made a conscious decision to change my thinking, which I choose to see as great progress versus a time when I didn't always learn quite so quickly.

I will make one confession about the day. The day after we returned home, we made a turkey for dinner!

Father God, thank you for another day. Every day, let us focus on all the blessings and good in our lives. It is up to us as to how we experience the day-to-day so we pay attention to the choices we make. We know it's up to us to see the good in every situation. When we look through eyes of love, we see good everywhere and in every person. Thank you, God. In Jesus' name, Amen.

Chapter 7

BELIEVE YOU WILL RECEIVE

Some time ago, I got to thinking that I wanted to start doing some kind of exercise program. I was walking my dog every day, but you don't get much exercise when the dog stops every few feet to sniff around. I was never big on exercising, but now that the idea had entered my mind, I seemed unable to get rid of it. I didn't know what I wanted to do, just something I could do at home whenever I could make the time. What I did know was that going to a gym was not for me.

Let me tell you what happened.

As the idea was still forming in my mind, I mentioned it to my friend, Nina. Just a couple of days later, literally two or three days, she called and started telling me about a walking program she was familiar with. It was on DVD and I could do it in my home, whenever I had the time. The best part was no special equipment was needed. I didn't even need to buy the DVDs; they were all available online. Perfect! This walking program turned out to be exactly what I was looking for.

I hadn't gotten very far in my thinking to define my desire; I just wanted something that would help me exercise, and I got it. By casually bringing it up one day, I had put it out to the universe, and the universe did the rest.

This wasn't something that I "sat down and seriously prayed about," but it was something that I felt was important for me to be doing. As I thought about it, it just felt like a prayer that hadn't been spoken out loud. Nevertheless, I do believe it was an answered prayer. Yes, it is a simple thing, and many times we may question what is and what is not appropriate to pray about. More importantly, I have seen that, as my relationship with God grows, it is in the day-to-day business of living that including God has brought me to that place of "being in the flow." Life is easier, more joyful, and more fun.

Father God, we open our hearts to You over every part of our lives, big or small, we want to include You in all we do. The more we share with You our everyday lives, the more we see Your hand involved in all we need. We thank You God for all the ways You show Your love for us, every day, all the time. In Jesus name we pray, Amen.

Chapter 8

ACCEPT WHO YOU ARE

Have you ever thought to yourself, "If I could just do it the way they do it," whatever "it" is, "my life would be better, and everything would work out perfectly?" Logically, we may know that, in most areas of life, there are many ways to do the same thing, none being right or wrong, just different. Yet, we tend to see our way as being "the wrong way." In the following story, I tell about an "aha" moment I experienced that, at first, felt almost silly to me. Yet, as time went by, I came to see its significance in many areas of my life. As most lessons turn out to be, this was a simple yet very important one for me, and a very common one. When we make an effort to be present as we go through our daily lives, opportunities for learning and growing will just show up. Our job is to be aware, take notice, and find the lesson.

I'll start at the beginning.

I want my yard to look as good as my neighbor's, but knowing what plants to buy and where to put them is not my strong suit, so I decided to ask my friend Nina for help.

Nina lives in a condo with a very small yard, which, to me, always looks picture-perfect. She seems to know the names of all the plants and flowers ever created. She knows exactly how to arrange the plantings in such a way that, along with her beautiful pots and other perfectly selected decorative items, makes her garden look like something you'd see in a magazine. I called and asked for help, and we picked a day for her to come over so we could make a plan.

As we looked around my yard, we decided to zero-in on two or three areas that needed special attention. We came up with a pretty good idea of what to buy to achieve the desired effect. So, off to the flower shops and nurseries we went. As we shopped, I noticed how Nina was able to focus on one thing at a time. She would look for one particular item until she found it—and she always found it.

I, on the other hand, had a different style. I looked everywhere at everything. I didn't want to miss anything, and I thought by looking around at everything, I might find that special something we hadn't thought of that would be just right. Or maybe I'd see something totally different that I might like more than the original plan. I felt I was being open to possibilities and found it all quite fun. There were a couple of times that Nina needed to rein me in and explain why some gorgeous plant I had just found wouldn't work. She was very patient as she reminded me that by living on a lake, which at times can be quite windy, I was limited to choosing plants that were hearty enough for that type of environment. After making two stops, we ended up going to one more nursery to find the last of what was needed to complete what I hoped would become a beautifully land-scaped yard.

After we returned to my house and started setting out where everything would go, I couldn't stop thinking about our plant excursion and the way we each shopped. We approached the whole project so very differently and were still able to find just what we needed, along with a couple of extra plants I just had to have.

Our different ways both worked to accomplish the goal of that day. This was becoming an "aha" moment for me. It suddenly dawned on me that the way I approach things is just fine. I can have fun in the moment, relax with whatever it is I'm doing, and stop comparing myself to others with the thought that their way is always better, and that I need to change. It was a message I had heard at least a thousand times before but this time I really did hear it, it had finally gotten through; it is okay to be myself, to have fun, and enjoy all that I am doing.

I have had experiences like this before, just going about my business in the normal activities of the day when some-thing electrifies my thoughts by shifting my perception. I find it all quite exciting! I was able see how this "aha" moment could carry over into other areas of my thinking. It helped me to understand that there is no reason to see myself as wrong just because I may do something differ-ently from someone else. This was big stuff for me! It can be pretty powerful to finally realize that I'm okay the way I am, and to stop comparing myself to others. This was not a new idea that I had never heard before, but I was finally able to really hear it, understand it, and see how to use it. Amazing!

Father God, I thank you today for the person You created me to be. I accept every part of who I am, a being with gifts and talents and a being with some less-than-perfect parts. When I accept the "all of me," I give myself the freedom to be who I am and to live with a deeper understanding of all of us. When I accept myself, I can break down my own walls and let the world in. Then I can help others see it is safe to break down their own walls. When we recognize we are all gifts to each other, it can have a profound effect on how we see the world. Thank you, God, for the gifts You have given each one of us. In Jesus' name, Amen.

Chapter 9

LET GOD WORK THROUGH YOU

Sometimes, God's voice can be so quiet, we're not sure if we really heard it. It can be an idea that comes into your mind for such a brief moment that we question if we heard anything. This following story is about just that: having an idea pop into your head, grasping it, and doing something with it.

My husband, Art, and I were in Florida when the recent Covid virus really started hitting the US. We usually go down for a couple of months to get away from the cold winters in Michigan. It was now around the beginning of April, and many states and cities—many countries, for that matter—had started enforcing a "stay at home" order and closing most businesses to try to stop the spread of the virus. At that point, doctors and scientists were still trying to understand the effects and symptoms of this new virus, who was being affected by it, and how it was being spread. It had caused many deaths worldwide, and trying to get it under control was proving to be quite a task. With even churches being closed, it was a difficult time, and I missed that sense of connectedness that comes from meeting together.

One morning, the idea came to me to write a little prayer of encouragement and text it out to a group of women I feel very close to at church. There are nine of us, and Clare, who is also a Prayer Chaplain and one of the group, has given us the name "Tea Party Society." A favorite pastime is having "high tea" and just spending time together. So, I got out my phone and composed a brief prayer simply stating how thankful we all are for each other and sent it out by text. I received comments back saying how much the prayer was appreciated. When I got up the next day, I wrote another, or I should say I started typing and spirit caused the words to just flow through me.

This became a daily practice. Every morning, I would send out a prayer. Sometimes the words and ideas would come to me the minute I woke up, and I found myself scrambling to get the words on paper, they would come so fast. I continued sending out prayers every morning.

There was one morning, I was running a little behind, and one of the girls sent a text saying, "Are you alright? I haven't received my prayer yet this morning." It became a wonderful and encouraging way we could stay connected during this difficult time. It all came about because I listened to that whisper of a voice that said, "Send out a prayer to the girls." By now, I have sent out a prayer every day since I started in April of 2020.

In addition, Mondays are our meditation days; the idea had come to me to send out a meditation on Mondays, instead of a prayer, and that is what I do. I send it out at about 8:00 in the morning, and if one of us can't do the meditation at that time, then we do it later in the day. It's still the idea that we're sharing this time together.

These prayers and meditations served a purpose for those who received them by being a bit of encouragement every day and keeping us connected during a very difficult time. At the same time, I had the wonderful experience of feeling that God was using me, if even in a small way, to be a source of light to others and to help us all know that we are not alone.

Father God, when I let go of my own thinking and let You work through me, my heart and mind begin to soar with a new boldness, a fearlessness that helps me believe anything is possible. New ideas start taking form, opening my mind beyond my usual way of thinking. Doubt is swept away, replaced with an inner knowing and assuredness that when I follow Your lead, the way will be made clear. This is experiencing living life with You; this is what my soul yearns for, a deep awareness, a feeling of such peace, it defies words. A knowing within that all is well. Thank you, God, in Jesus' name, Amen.

Chapter 10

DAILY PRAYERS

As I mentioned in the previous story, Mondays were the only day I didn't send out a prayer. I had been given the idea to send out a meditation on Mondays, so that is what I would do.

So, on one particular Monday, I had sent out the meditation by email and had texted everyone that it had been sent, just like I normally do every Monday. A few minutes later, ideas for a new prayer started coming to me, and at first I thought this could be a prayer to use the next day. It didn't happen very often, maybe only a couple of times before, that I would prepare a prayer ahead of time. My usual routine would be writing out a prayer while having my early morning cup of tea, so I decided to type it out and save it on my computer. I had started saving all the prayers I had been sending out, dating, and saying in a few words the gist of each one. By my count today, I have now sent out over eight hundred prayers and have quite a collection. I often go back and reread them and find much encouragement from the words God blessed me with.

Now, back to the story.

As I was writing, the thought kept coming to me to text something out to the girls that day, something that some-one needed to hear. Every day, after a prayer had been sent, comments would be shared, such as "Amen" or "So true." And at least once a week, someone would let it be known how much they needed those words that day. As I continued typing, the thought came through so clearly to go ahead and send this prayer out that day, and so, that's what I did. I trust that still, small voice and follow what it tells me. As I was typing out the text, I had a sense that it would be one of those days when someone would comment, "I really needed to hear this today," and that is exactly what happened.

If we are open to it, God will use us in the most amazing ways. We do not have to be perfect or especially qualified; God will qualify those He uses. Sending out daily prayers has been as much of a blessing to me as it is to those who receive them.

Father God, this is the start of another "day the Lord has made," a gift from You. Do we see it that way? Do we treasure every day we are given? Do we use each day wisely? You, God, have given each of us gifts and talents; these gifts are not meant just for us but also as blessings to others. Show us Your way for us, how we can share all that we are blessed with. Help us keep our hearts and minds open to Your direction so that we may be a blessing to others. This is what we ask for today and every day. Thank You God. In Jesus' name we pray, Amen.

Chapter 11

PRAY ABOUT
EVERYDAY LIFE

It was a Friday night, and Art and I were leaving for a business trip in six days. I was wanting to get my hair done before we left, but Connie, who usually does my hair, had left for vacation and would not be back until after we left. My sister, who has been a hairdresser for years, said, "Not to worry; I'll do your hair." There is a reason my sister no longer does my hair. She used to do it on a regular basis, but a few years ago when we were getting ready to go on another business trip, it had been difficult to fit me into her schedule. It wasn't until midnight, the night before we were leaving, that she ended up doing my hair with a cut and color. I was glad it worked out, but it was a bit "hair-raising" having to wait until the last minute.

Now, you may be wondering, "How could this possibly have anything to do with prayer?" I'll explain.

So, as I was saying: up to this point, we still hadn't worked out when she would be available, and past experience was rearing its ugly head. What if it turns out like before, with her doing my hair at midnight? What if it turns out she can't do it at all? I had to stop myself right there. This kind of thinking was not helping. I took a minute to calm down and breathe and think about what I really needed to happen here, and that is what I prayed about. I asked that things would go smoothly and that I would get what I needed. I also prayed that my mind would be open to any possibility.

After a little time passed, an idea came to me: call the shop where Connie works and see if someone could fit me in. Okay, finally, some logic. I called first thing the next morning and explained my situation. Yes, there had been a cancellation that morning. If I could be there in an hour, David could do my hair. This was perfect; Connie had told me the color I would need, and they had it at the shop. But then I remembered that for a part of the coloring process I needed a different brand from the one provided with the color. I knew they sold it at one of the local supply stores, so I started getting ready as my husband went online to see if there could possibly be one on my way to the salon. Yes, there was one right on the way; I would have time to stop and pick it up and not be late. I hurried myself along and got out the door in record time.

When I got to the supply shop, there was a sign on the door that read "temporarily closed." I couldn't believe it; up until now, everything had gone so well. I continued on to the hair salon, all the time thinking, "They'll have something else they can use; I just trust it will turn out alright." I arrived at the shop right on time, and David was ready. I explained my dilemma about needing a different product from the one provided. He said, "No problem, we have just what you need." He was so happy with how the color turned out he said he'd start using this other product on his own clients. It had worked well and was also less expensive. It turned out that David and I knew many of the same people, so we had quite a visit, talking the whole time I was there.

Such a simple, everyday thing, needing to get my hair done. What made it different was I chose to stop and ask God, acknowledging my need for help, and my prayer was answered!

Father God, Scripture tells us "We don't have because we don't ask." What is in my heart that I am not asking for? And why? Why am I not asking? We may believe that all of our daily needs will be met, but what about the secret desires of the heart? Do I believe You will give me what I desire? Have I ever asked or talked with You about what I would like in my life? It is up to me to ask, and the time is now. You have planted these desires in our hearts; if they were not possible, they wouldn't be there. So, this day, I take time to go within and search my own heart and reveal to myself what I want, and then open up to You and give it over to You. Thank you, God, that You are in my life. We offer this prayer in Jesus' name, Amen.

Chapter 12

GOD IS THE SOURCE OF YOUR NEW IDEA

This story is about the power of setting an intention. Let me explain.

I am not a person that runs to the doctor for every ache and pain, but I do go in for a yearly check-up just to keep an eye on things. My doctor will usually do bloodwork along with whatever else he feels necessary.

One particular year, the results from a thyroid test he had done showed very low levels, which caused him to suggest using medication to bring my thyroid levels back up to normal. It took quite a while to come up with the right dosage. When I took the higher dosage, which the bloodwork indicated was needed, I didn't feel well, but when I would take a lower dosage, it wasn't enough to bring the levels up to where they should be. This went on for over two years, cutting the dosage back and then trying to increase the amount slowly so my body could adjust. I had gone such a long time with the levels being at such a low count, it was hard for my body to get used to the change the medication was trying to make.

It was becoming very frustrating, as all this was happening, and I wasn't feeling any better. I kept thinking, "What can I do to help myself?" And then it came to me that, with this medication, my body may need to go through an adjustment period, that maybe if I could just tough it out and take the higher dose for a couple weeks, I could get through the adjustment time, and all would be well.

As that thought was forming, another thought came. It occurred to me to call the pharmacist and explain the situation and get his opinion. He was very helpful as I explained my story, and he confirmed there can be an adjustment period with this medication. Once I got off the phone, I decided right then and there that I would tough it out for two weeks and see how I felt. I was determined that I would get through this, even if I had to fight my way through. My mind was made up, so I started the higher dose the next day and never looked back.

The problems I had experienced in the past from increasing the dosage never came back. From that day forward, the symptoms that had plagued me for almost two years were gone. Hallelujah!

When thoughts or ideas come to us, I believe that is one way God uses to answer our prayers. It is up to us to follow through. When we give the credit to God, we are acknowledging Him in our lives. We are saying, "Yes, God is working in my life." Wow!

Father God, we ask that You direct our steps, and it is up to us to recognize that You are doing just that. The path we are on is guided by You, the thoughts and ideas we have are given to us by You. That is how You direct our steps, and the more we see You at work in our lives, the more open we become to walking in Your way. It is both exhilarating and a little unnerving to accept that You are involved in each one of our lives. How blessed we are to really feel Your presence. Thank you, God; thank you, God. In Jesus' name we pray, Amen.

Chapter 13

ENJOY THE WONDER ALL AROUND YOU

I am a shell-seeker. Over the years, when a business trip or personal travel would take us near the ocean, at the first opportunity, I would be heading to the beach, looking for shells. I find shells to be among the most beautiful and intricate of God's creations. Their colors and shapes and amazing designs fill me with joy as I search the sand. This particular story happened when I was in Naples, Florida. Art, and I have a condo there, and yes, I have many jars of shells throughout the house. The following is about the time I wanted to find a sand dollar.

Walking the beach alone, just wandering to my heart's content, is one of my favorite pastimes. It is part of my spiritual practice whenever I am near the water. I know this sounds so cliche, but the rush of the waves overtaking the quiet, and the occasional dolphin swimming off in the distance just thrills my soul. I find immense joy in just walking along and searching the sand for shells. Large, small, every color, shells fascinate me with their beauty.

On this particular day, the thought crossed my mind that it would be amazing to find a whole sand dollar. They can be found, but by the time they make it to shore, most are usually broken up into many pieces. So, as I walked with the warm sand seeping between my toes and the heat of the sun soothing my body, I felt completely content just being there. Every few feet, I would stop and check out a shell half-buried in the sand, hoping it would be a beauty.

As I was looking down, a man I had not noticed before walked right up to me with a netted bag in his hand, carrying the treasures he had found that day. He took out a piece of coral to show me and was explaining how he would dive just a few yards out and find the most wonderful shells and coral. It was then that I noticed the sand dollar lying at the bottom of his bag. It was perfect, beautiful in its design and shape, completely whole. Without a word, he reached deep into the bag, brought it out and gave it to me! I was stunned and so excited; a complete stranger walks up to me out of the blue and hands me what I had just been thinking about a little while before. After that, he just walked away as I stood there convinced that I had drawn him to me with my thoughts about sand dollars. Some might say it was just coincidence; I see it as another time the abundant universe brought me what I wanted.

Father God, it can be so easy to lose our sense of wonder as we go about our daily lives, but today I choose to see the world through the eyes of a child. I choose to be amazed at what we call the simple things, to open my eyes and see anew. Life can be an adventure if we choose to look at it with excitement, with the idea of what I can learn today. Our attitude determines the degree of joy or lack of joy we experience every day, so let us start each day with fresh eyes and see what the world wants to bring us. Thank you, God, that we are open to finding joy in every situation. We offer this prayer in Jesus' name, Amen.

Chapter 14

CHANGE YOUR THOUGHTS, CHANGE YOUR LIFE

I have in my head what I call a "continual prayer" of being open to any "aha" moments or times of consciousness when a learning experience is happening. The following story is one such time.

As I said, Art and I have a condo down in Naples, Florida. It's a beautiful area, and we often invite friends and family to come and visit while we're there during the cold winter months. This particular year, we had already hosted three groups of visitors, and a whole new batch were due to start arriving the following week.

Art has three grown daughters from a previous marriage. The oldest, Tricia, has five children, and they were all heading down, starting with Jenna, Tricia's oldest daughter, and a friend. They would be visiting for a week. The last day of their visit would be the day when Tricia, her husband and two more daughters, ages seven and three, were set to arrive. The four of them would be staying for eight days. Jenna and her friend would leave, and two days later, her two older brothers would be coming for five days while the rest of the family was still with us—Whew!

We had just packed off our latest guests, and it was a few days before this whole bunch would be descending on our two-bedroom condo. I know, hard to keep it all straight.

As I was taking my daily beach walk and talking with God one morning, I had one of those "aha" moments. As much as I enjoy having company, I realized I was almost dreading the arrival of our next guests. I found myself laughing out loud as I finally acknowledged this to myself.

We had been so busy, and the thought of people coming and going, the need to feed all these people, and the idea of no privacy had been swirling in my mind. It also occurred to me that I had been wanting a little time without constantly having people around. I am a "people person," yet I am also one who needs a good amount of "quiet time."

It was finally getting through to me that I had been projecting and setting up, in my mind, how difficult the next two weeks were going to be. I was stunned. Talk about not living in the present. I was laughing at myself again; I thought I knew this stuff.

So, there I was, walking on the beach, talking out loud to God, and laughing. What a sight. I stopped my thinking right there and took a moment to realize that this "aha" moment was an answer to a continual prayer for direction, understanding, and awareness in how I live my life. So, I did literally stop walking, and then took a few minutes to "choose" how I wanted the next few weeks to be.

I made a conscious decision to … *stop filling my mind with thoughts that were not helping me!* I replaced them with thoughts of how well this would go and the fun we would have, and to stop my mind from thinking—or should I say, "planning," for all the difficulties that might come up. It took a little doing, and I had to repeatedly catch my thinking, really, being aware of the direction my mind was going and change it when needed. I also was able to remember that our building has two suites that owners can rent for extra guests, and we were able to reserve one for several nights to ease some of the congestion in the condo I had been fearing.

Taking the time to look at my thinking really made a difference in how the time actually turned out: fun for all.

Father God, our minds are capable of being in the past with wonderful memories or being in the future dreaming of how we would like things to be. But help us to stay present to the now, living our lives now. To live in the moment and experience life as it is happening can sometimes take effort, but it is always worth it. To be aware to enjoying life now with all its precious moments is a gift to cherish. We thank You God for this life today. This we pray in Jesus' name, Amen.

Chapter 15

BELIEVE GOD HAS A PLAN FOR YOU

The desire to help the church in a financial way came to me one day after I had been working in the church office. I am a Prayer Chaplain, and I often spend time in the office updating the log sheets that we use to make our wellness calls and whatever else needs to be done to keep things running smoothly. One day while there, I was talking with CJ, a full-time volunteer, who keeps things up and running in the church office. The building had been put up for sale, and we wondered who might buy it.

This led to a discussion about Jack Boland, who had started Renaissance Unity/Church of Today, and how different things had become. I had not attended the church when Jack Boland had been there, and I had never heard any of his talks, even though they had all been recorded. It had been over twenty years since his death, and people were still raving about what an amazing speaker he was. They still marveled at the countless numbers who had been helped by his messages and kindness.

CJ would often receive calls from people asking if Jack's speeches were for sale. The master recordings were still there, but no one was available to make copies, and most people wanted CDs or a file to download from the internet. That night, I received the answer to my desire. This is how it happened.

That evening, as I was working on my latest quilt, an idea came to me: what if I could help in some way to make Jack Boland's talks available again? I hadn't been thinking about the earlier conversation with CJ. I was just sitting there, sewing away, and this just popped into my head. Could this bring extra income to the church? I was excited; my mind exploded with ideas and possibilities. I was planning to work at the church the next day and decided to share my idea with CJ, or to be more precise, the idea that God had placed in my mind. I rushed to the church the next morning. I truly believed this came from God, and I had no doubt that something wonderful and exciting was taking root.

CJ was already there when I burst through the door and jumped right in to tell her about this idea. As it turned out, I was not the only one interested in doing something with this wealth of information. She, too, had thought many times that there must be some way to make use of years of recordings. Sunday sermons, workshops and classes, whole series of discussions covering dozens of topics, all just sitting on shelves, waiting to be heard again. She was onboard and knew the next step: we would approach the church CEO regarding the subject. It was hard to contain our excitement as she called him and set up an appointment for the following week. In the back of my mind, I had been wanting another project to work on. This could be it!

Our meeting with the CEO was another example of how God works to bring people together with a shared goal. He was well aware of the value the church had in these hundreds of talks. Not only were there talks by Jack Boland, but, over the years, there had been dozens of guest speakers, all of whom had been recorded: Wayne Dyer, Les Brown, Father Leo Booth, Edwene Gaines, Ernie Larsen, Deepak Chopra. These were just a few of the many speakers who had shared their knowledge and years of learning at this church. Unbeknownst to us, the CEO had been waiting for the right people to come forward and tackle this immense task. He gave us the go-ahead, and we were both elated!

I started the next day by taking a look at the duplication and storage rooms where many of the cassettes and CDs were kept. It was a mess. It had not only become a storage room for the church food pantry, but also a place to put things that were no longer used. I had my work cut out for me.

The first step would be taking an inventory and listing what could be hundreds of talks. Then I would create and implement some kind of organized system. This was right up my alley. I love doing this kind of work, and it didn't feel daunting to me at all.

I found it to be a wonderful confirmation of what I've heard many times, that God is working behind the scenes to bring the right people together to accomplish a shared purpose. There is no end to the ways God can use us if we are open and willing to hear His direction.

Father God, we come to times in our lives that become major turning points, a shift happens, and a new direction or a new way of thinking opens up. These can be gifts from You, moving us past our own thinking. When we trust in Your wisdom, we know we can't go wrong, and we thank You God that Your way is our best way. This we pray in Jesus' name, Amen.

Chapter 16

LEARN FROM EVERY SITUATION

We can learn anytime, anywhere, if we choose to pay attention to the lessons God is giving us. It's all in what we *want* to see. This next story is about such a situation.

I was returning home from the plant nursery, feeling good. I had been looking for a couple of "porch pots" already filled with plants and flowers, ready to go. Every year, I buy two matching pots to set on my front porch just to make the house look pretty. It was late in the year, and all the really pretty ones had already been sold. The only ones left at the places I had already been to were the leftovers nobody wanted, but lo and behold, I found two that were perfect for me. And yes, I had prayed about it before I left on my shopping trip that day. Once I arrived home, all I had to do was flip open the back of my SUV, set them strategically on the porch, and presto! My house would be lookin' good.

But I wasn't home yet. I was at an intersection, waiting for the red light to change, when there was a truck pulling out of the corner gas station, wanting to make a left turn. I held back so he would be able to make his turn in front of me as soon as the light changed to green, and the car in front of me moved forward so this truck could fit between us. The light finally changed to green, but the car in front seemed to be taking its good old time to start moving. The man in the truck was shaking his fist in the air as he glared at the car for not moving. After just a moment, which seemed like forever, the car moved and the man in the truck was able to go off on his un-merry way.

I found it amusing that he was so upset at that car he felt was holding him back, yet he didn't seem to notice that I was trying to help him by making sure he would have the needed space to make his turn.

It made me wonder about how many times I might have done the same type of thing: being so focused on the problem and, at the same time, missing the good that was happening around me. It helped me to see the importance of paying attention, to look for the good in my life, everywhere, all the time.

Father God, we are always ready to learn something new, to explore a new way or try new ideas. Finding excitement in new accomplishments and expanding our world keeps us growing and is nourishment to our souls. We thank You God that we were created to continually learn. In Jesus' name we pray, Amen.

Chapter 17

DON'T BE AFRAID TO ASK

I've had pets all my life; they were part of my growing up. My memories of childhood revolve around the many cats and dogs that were part of our family. I've had a steady stream of dogs all of my adult life, and the one I had at the time of this story was named Sadie.

Sadie was a rescued dog, as most of my pets have been. She was found in a dumpster, starving and weak, and was taken to the Humane Society. After examining her, it was discovered that she'd had a litter of puppies, but they were nowhere to be found. She entered my life a few months after my previous dog passed on, and she filled my life with love.

The following story is about her miracle.

Sadie had a deformed front leg, which had always caused her some difficulty walking, but on one particular day, something more was happening. As I was watching her outside, she didn't seem to have any control of her hind legs. The back end of her body seemed to be swaying, and her hind legs would just give out. My husband, Art, and I decided to take her to an emergency vet.

The first vet we went to didn't seem to know what the cause could be, so we left there and took her to another.

The second vet discovered she had two herniated discs in her neck and arthritis in her back. These two issues were probably causing the problems with her walking, and most likely, causing extreme pain. She was put on many pain medications, which didn't seem to help, and walking became almost impossible.

I took her to our regular vet clinic, and they didn't have any better answers than to keep her on pain medications. They had no hope of her ever walking normally again.

It was breaking my heart to see this happening to her, but I didn't know what to do. I prayed about how to help her and asked for guidance in what should be my next step.

For my own health care, I am a believer in alternative methods and holistic modalities of healing, so I decided to see what I could come up with for Sadie. A friend of mine is a certified practitioner of Cranial Sacral, which deals with issues of the spine. I decided to approach her to see if she knew of someone who used it on dogs. She said she would do some checking and get back to me. Her contact was not aware of anyone working with dogs, which was very disappointing. I just couldn't believe there was nothing I could do. I'd had this dog for eleven years; she was a part of my everyday life, and I felt I had to keep trying. I again prayed for guidance and was given the idea of trying acupuncture.

I knew, right then, this was the next step, but had no idea how to find the best place to take her. I decided to try looking online. One place seemed to "jump" out at me. I called and explained Sadie's situation and the doctor thought they could help her. I had mentioned all of this to a friend and discovered she had taken her dog to this same vet and was very impressed by how they treated her dog. I called to make an appointment, and they were able to take her that same week.

I was very excited as we walked in the door for her first appointment. The vet was kind, patient, and very gentle as she worked with Sadie, finding just the right spot to place the acupuncture needles. It didn't take long to see that this was working. After just three treatments, Sadie could walk! She was wobbly at first, but when I compare this to the times I would watch her trying to walk and having to drag her hind legs, I was ecstatic. I continued taking her, and with every treatment, she improved. After a total of just six treatments, she was back to running. Running! My vet was so impressed with what she saw happening with Sadie that she recommended acupuncture for some of her other patients with similar issues.

Father God, we can find joy in the simplest things, in the beauty and fun that are all around us. We also find this joy in our pets that become part of the family, that comfort us with their love and their ability to seem to understand people. What an amazing gift You have given us with animals. We thank You God for the part they play in adding so much love to our lives. This we pray in Jesus' name, Amen.

In closing, I hope this book has given you a lot to think about as you walk your own path. Use these stories to help you remember your own experiences, maybe a time when just the right answer came to you seemingly out of nowhere. Ask God for His help and you'll be amazed at what can happen. God is waiting for us to invite Him in and if we do, it truly can change your life.